The Art of Mindful Priorities: Transform Your Life by Embracing Mindful Priorities

Table of Contents:

Chapter 1

Introduction: The Myth of Caring About Everything

Dear reader

In the rushing about of our cutting edge lives, there's a predominant thought that we ought to be equipped for taking care of everything tossed our direction. We are encouraged to multitask, juggling multiple obligations, ambitions, and responsibilities simultaneously. The outcome? A mind-boggling feeling of pressure that frequently leaves us feeling excessively slim, battling to stay aware of the determined requests around us.

This determined quest for "thinking often about everything" can be exhausting. It's like attempting to clutch a modest bunch of sand - the more we attempt to get a handle on, the more gets past us. We've been adapted to accept that being useful means doing everything, being all over the place, and accomplishing everything at the same time.

However, in the midst of this disarray, there lies a strong cure: careful prioritization.

Envision an alternate methodology, one where rather than spreading ourselves meagerly across everything, we center around the main thing. Careful prioritization urges us to stop, calmly inhale, and pose ourselves a critical inquiry: What genuinely merits our time, consideration, and energy?

It's tied in with recognizing that we can't do everything. All things being equal, it's tied in with picking where to coordinate our endeavors, deliberately and intentionally. This doesn't mean forsaking liabilities; rather, it implies understanding that not all things hold equivalent significance in our lives.

Careful prioritization isn't just about making a plan for the day or booking errands; It's a fundamental mental shift. It's an acknowledgement that if we focus on a few important things, we can do well in them. Thusly, we make the way for a more significant and satisfying presence.

Consider this methodology as a solution for the legend of "thinking often about everything." It resembles cleaning up the brain, eliminating the pointless commotion and focusing on the tunes that really resound with our spirits. It's enabling on the grounds that it permits us to recover our organization over our lives, directing our decisions in view of what lines up with our qualities, goals, and prosperity.

The simplicity of mindful prioritization is what makes it appealing. There's actually no need to focus on adding more undertakings to a generally spilling over plan for the day;

it's tied in with being conscious in our decisions, zeroing in on what gives us pleasure, satisfaction, and a feeling of direction.

This presentation fills in as a greeting — a cancel to step the treadmill of vast errands and responsibilities and enter a domain where quality outperforms amount. As a means of navigating our complex and fast-paced world with greater ease, balance, and contentment, it is a call to embrace mindful prioritization.

Let's explore the transformative power of mindful prioritization in shaping a life that is not just about doing everything but also about doing what truly matters as we embark on this journey together.

Chapter 2

Understanding Your Priorities: The Power of Selective Attention

In the clamoring mosaic of current presence, our consideration is persistently requested from all corners. The power of particular consideration arises as a priceless compass in the midst of this chaos, directing us toward soundness, reason, and a feeling of grounded clearness.

At its center, particular consideration comprises a cognizant and conscious demonstration, a long way past the simple prohibition of interruptions. It addresses a careful curation of our psychological scene — a purposeful decision to dispense our mental assets toward components reverberating with our most profound qualities, desires, and prosperity. This figurative spotlight, when capably used, enlightens the forms of importance inside the tremendous material of our lives.

This excursion into understanding the strength of a specific center isn't simply a challenge to isolate components in light of their obvious significance; it's a significant assessment of our sense of direction. It urges us to strip back the layers of cultural molding and friend past the constant fuss for our consideration. Through this reflective journey, we recognize that few out of every odd interest justifies an equivalent portion of our psychological data transmission. We understand that by deliberately adjusting our regard for our inborn qualities and certified desires, we set out on a groundbreaking excursion toward purposeful living.

Inside the hallways of this investigation, we adventure into the core of acumen — a perplexing course of refining that isolates the fundamental from the unimportant in the midst of the ceaseless flood of improvements. We examine the repercussions of our choices and their tangible impact on the tapestry of our day-to-day experiences here, engrossing ourselves in profound introspection. Through a progression of intelligent activities and provocative requests, we furnish ourselves with the key instruments important to explore the maze of consideration and deliberateness.

The dominance of specific consideration isn't just an expertise; it's a door to a more significant and deliberate presence. As we participate in the specialty of deliberately coordinating our concentration, we shape a daily existence where each picked feature enhances the extravagance and profundity of our encounters, contributing definitively to our all encompassing prosperity.

Take this transformative journey with me through "The Art of Mindful Priorities"'s realms. How about we disentangle the woven artwork of purposeful living by embracing the significant impact of directing our consideration intentionally toward what genuinely reverberates with the pith of what our identity is and what we try to turn into.

Absolutely, focusing on what truly matters is pivotal for a fulfilled life. Here are the critical points:

Significance of Focusing on What Truly Matters:

1. Clarity in Direction: Identifying what truly matters provides a roadmap for life. It gives a clear direction, guiding decisions and actions towards meaningful goals.

2. Reduced Stress and Overwhelm:When attention is directed towards essentials, it minimizes distractions and reduces the feeling of being overwhelmed by trivial matters.

3. Enhanced Productivity and Efficiency:By focusing on core priorities, energy and effort are concentrated where they make the most significant impact, resulting in enhanced productivity.

4. Greater Fulfillment: Aligning actions with core values and goals leads to a sense of fulfillment and purpose, fostering a deeper sense of contentment in life.

Practical Tips to Identify and Prioritize Core Values and Goals:

1.   Self-Reflection:Spend time in introspection to understand personal values and what truly matters. What brings joy, fulfillment, and a sense of purpose?

2. Define Values:List down core values – integrity, family, personal growth, etc. Evaluate how current activities align with these values.

3. Set Clear Goals:Define specific, achievable, and measurable goals in various aspects of life: career, relationships, health, and personal growth.

4. Prioritization Matrix:Use tools like a priority matrix (e.g., Eisenhower Matrix) to categorize tasks based on importance and urgency. This aids in focusing on high-value tasks.

5. Saying No: Learn to say no to commitments that don't align with core values or goals. It creates space for what truly matters.

6. Regular Review: Revisit and reassess priorities periodically. Life is dynamic; priorities may shift, and that's okay. Regular evaluation ensures alignment.

7. Mindfulness Practices: Techniques like meditation, journaling, or mindfulness

exercises can help gain clarity on what truly matters by quieting external noise.

8. Seek Guidance: Discuss priorities with trusted friends, mentors, or coaches. External perspectives can shed light on blind spots and offer valuable insights.

9. Start Small: Begin with a few priorities to avoid feeling overwhelmed. As habits form, gradually incorporate more.

By focusing on what truly matters—aligning actions with core values and goals—we pave the way for a more purposeful and fulfilling life. The journey involves introspection, setting clear priorities, and making conscious choices in line with these priorities. This intentional approach allows us to channel our time and energy into endeavors that truly resonate with our essence, fostering a life rich in meaning and fulfillment.

Chapter 3

Embracing Imperfection: Letting Go of Unrealistic Expectations

In the pursuit of success, happiness, and fulfillment, we often fall into the trap of chasing perfection. We set sky-high standards for ourselves in various facets of life, expecting flawlessness in our work, relationships, appearance, and achievements. However, this quest for perfection is often futile, leading to stress, anxiety, and a sense of inadequacy.

Embracing imperfection involves recognizing and accepting our inherent human nature—the beauty in our flaws, mistakes, and shortcomings. It's about acknowledging that perfection is an unrealistic ideal, and the pursuit of it can be both draining and demoralizing.

This idea of imperfection as a catalyst for personal growth is pivotal in the realm of mindful priorities. When we let go of unrealistic expectations, a profound transformation occurs:

Relieving the Burden of Expectations

1. Authentic Self-Acceptance:Embracing imperfection allows us to embrace our authentic selves. It fosters self-compassion and self-acceptance, acknowledging that it's okay not to have everything figured out.

2. Reduced Stress and Anxiety:Releasing the burden of unrealistic expectations alleviates stress and anxiety associated with trying to meet unattainable standards. It liberates us from the constant pressure to be flawless in every aspect of life.

3. Freedom to Explore and Experiment: Embracing imperfection creates space for experimentation and exploration. It encourages risk-taking and innovation without the fear of failure.

Greater Satisfaction and Fulfillment

1.   Emotional   Well-being: Accepting imperfection fosters a more positive mindset. It allows us to find joy in progress rather than solely in achieving perfection.

2. Enhanced Relationships:Letting go of unrealistic expectations in relationships cultivates understanding and empathy. It encourages acceptance of others' imperfections, strengthening connections.

3. Improved Productivity: Instead of obsessing over perfection, focusing on progress and iteration can lead to more productive outcomes. It fosters a growth-oriented mindset where learning from mistakes is valued.

Mindful Priorities in Imperfection

Relating back to the essence of the book on mindful priorities, embracing imperfection plays a crucial role. It's about understanding that setting mindful priorities doesn't mean flawlessness in execution. Instead, it involves acknowledging imperfections and choosing to direct efforts towards what truly matters despite these imperfections.

By integrating imperfection into the concept of mindful prioritization, individuals can craft a more compassionate and realistic approach to setting and pursuing their priorities. It allows for a more forgiving attitude towards oneself and others, fostering a mindset that values progress over perfection.

In essence, the art of mindful priorities involves embracing imperfection as an integral part of the journey. It's about recognizing the beauty in imperfection, allowing it to fuel personal growth, and ultimately leading to greater satisfaction and fulfillment in the pursuit of what truly matters.

Chapter 4

Choosing Your Battles: The Art of Effective Decision-Making

Absolutely, decision-making is the cornerstone of our lives, influencing our paths, priorities, and outcomes. Here's an in-depth exploration of the importance of decision-making and strategies for mindful choices:

Importance of Decision-Making in Shaping Our Lives

Every day, we are confronted with choices—some trivial, others monumental. Decisions, both big and small, shape the trajectory of our lives. The significance of decision-making lies not just in the choices themselves but in their cumulative effect, gradually molding our experiences, opportunities, and priorities.

1. Life Path:Decisions steer us along certain paths, influencing our careers, relationships, and personal development. Whether it's choosing a career, a life partner, or where to live, decisions have a profound impact on our journey.

2. Resource Allocation:Decision-making involves allocating limited resources—time, energy, and money. Effective decisions optimize these resources, directing them towards what matters most.

3. Values Alignment:Decisions often reflect our values. Aligning choices with our core values leads to a more fulfilling and purpose-driven life.

4. Adaptability:Decision-making fosters adaptability. It allows us to pivot, learn from outcomes, and adjust our course based on new information or changing circumstances.

Strategies for Informed and Mindful Decision-Making

1. **Clarity of Priorities:** Define your priorities clearly. Understand what truly matters to you. This clarity becomes the compass guiding decision-making.

2. **Gather Information:** Base decisions on well-informed insights. Collect relevant data, seek advice, and consider various perspectives before reaching a conclusion.

3. **Assess Risks and Benefits:** Evaluate potential risks and benefits associated with each choice. This assessment helps in weighing the consequences against the desired outcomes.

4. **Use Decision-Making Models:** Utilize decision-making models like SWOT analysis, pros and cons lists, or decision matrices. These tools provide a structured approach to evaluating options.

5. **Listen to Intuition:** Trust your intuition. Sometimes, our instincts can offer valuable insights that rational analysis might miss.

6. **Practice Mindfulness:** Cultivate mindfulness in decision-making. Be present, aware, and conscious of the impact of choices on your life and others'.

7. **Embrace Flexibility:** Be open to adapt. Not all decisions yield the expected results. Embrace flexibility to recalibrate when needed.

8. **Set Decision-Making Criteria:** Establish criteria for your decisions based on values and long-term goals. This ensures alignment with your priorities.

9. **Reflect and Learn:** Review past decisions. Understand what worked and

what didn't. Learning from previous choices enhances future decision-making.

Alignment with Mindful Priorities

The art of effective decision-making intertwines seamlessly with the concept of mindful priorities. It's about making choices that align with your identified priorities, ensuring that every decision contributes positively to the life you envision.

By integrating mindful decision-making into the framework of mindful priorities, individuals can navigate the complexities of life with a clearer sense of direction and purpose. It allows for a deliberate and conscious approach to choices, ensuring that each decision supports the fulfillment of identified priorities.

7 Tips To Choose Your Battles (and Win Them)

Choosing your battles comes down to knowing when to take on a conflict and when to turn away. This means knowing how to assess the problem and evaluating the costs vs. benefits to decide whether to fight it. Here are my 7 tips to choose your battles and win them.

1) Evaluate the conflict

When you are presented with a conflict, ask yourself:

- How important is addressing this?
- What is the payoff from winning this? *(Is there an actual result to gain or is it for the sake of winning?)*

- Can my time be better spent elsewhere? *(Is there an opportunity cost of your time?)*

Often, the disagreements we face in life are trivial disputes with no consequence in the long run. Such as arguments with unreasonable or negative people. Engaging with them takes up our time and energy, distracts us from what's important, and disrupts our peace of mind. In such cases, it may be better to ignore them.

Once I was backstabbed by someone whom I thought was a friend. He said false and vindictive things about me in front of a business acquaintance. As the acquaintance knew me and knew that what the friend said was untrue, he told me about it, which was how I found out about what happened.

After initially feeling upset about it, I decided to let it go and cut the "friend" out of my life. While I could have confronted him, I realized that this friend constantly engaged in low-consciousness behavior throughout our short friendship, such as creating conflicts and arguments. I wasn't interested in any more drama and had other things to worry about.

Similarly, I've been in situations with unreasonable people where I decided it was better to turn away than argue or fight. Many times it's just a petty conflict and it's best to let go. Sometimes the end outcome — scoring a victory over someone unreasonable — is too trivial to justify picking a fight. The time spent engaging with the person, as well as the emotional energy expended, could be better spent elsewhere. Walking away isn't cowardice or weakness. **Sometimes walking away is a sign of strength and wisdom.**

Even when we choose not to fight, learn from the experience. For example, avoiding the person if we know him/her, and watching out for his/her antics. When we decide not to fight, we're not letting others walk over us. We're simply picking the higher ground and protecting our space and well-being.

2) Do a cost-benefit analysis

In the investment world, cost-benefit analysis is a systematic approach to determine the costs and benefits of a business investment and decide if it is sound. When faced with a conflict, do a cost-benefit analysis to help you decide if the battle is worth fighting. Ask yourself:

- What are the costs and benefits of fighting this battle?

- Do the costs outweigh the benefits? *(If so, it's generally better to let go and move on.)*

- What are the odds of success? *(If the odds of success are very low, it may be better to move on as well.)*

A few years ago, I signed a contract with a company to produce a product. After putting aside all my projects and dedicating a good half of the year to work on this, I successfully delivered the product and received great reviews from customers.

However, while this company was supposed to market the product, they stopped supporting it after a while without informing me. When I followed up on this matter — multiple times — they promised to do something but nothing was ever done. The contractual clauses relinquished my selling rights (we had a profit-sharing arrangement), and since they were supposed to market the product but backed out of the arrangement, it put me in a losing deal because I had invested my time into creating a high-quality product that I couldn't sell myself.

While I was peeved initially, especially when the company went dark in my attempts to follow up, I decided not to pursue the matter.

The reason is that even though the company is clearly at fault, there was little for me to gain in pursuing this further. Firstly, the company had already gone dark on me, which meant that any further attempts to pursue the matter would be difficult. Secondly, I didn't want to burn bridges (or whatever was left) by going down the scorched-earth path. Thirdly, even if I had my way and the company reinstated marketing support, it would have increased my revenue by five percent at most. For me, it was easier to achieve this goal by launching a new product (that I would have full rights to), rather than trying to force a response out of this company.

Does this mean that we should avoid all battles if there is little to no chance of success? No, not at all. Sometimes you want to fight a battle to make a statement and be heard.

For example, in the case of molestation, workplace harassment, bullying, or even medical negligence, you want to report the issue to raise awareness and stand up for yourself. I have personally reported school bullies before, and likewise workplace harassment. In the case of school bullies, their behaviors were corrected by the teacher, while a manager spoke to the workplace harasser.

The benefit of engaging in the battle doesn't have to be monetary — it can be a moral one, like protecting your rights, preventing further recurrence of the problem, and helping others. However you may be in a system that's broken or works against you — if so the better option may be to let go. Every situation is different, so weigh the costs and benefits before deciding what to do.

3) Go for win-win, not win-lose

Should you decide to take on the battle, create **a win-win where both of you will be victorious**.

Some of you may be surprised by my suggestion. *Why 'win-win' and not 'win-lose'? Why help my opponent win?* you may think.

Even though I use "battle" as the analogy, I encourage you to think about your "opponent" as your ally, your friend. The reason is simple: When you have a mindset to squash others, you adopt a scarcity mindset that's rooted in lack — where there must always be a winner and a loser, where one must always supersede another. The truth is there are often enough opportunities to go around, and everyone can win together.

This comes from having an abundance mindset first. Not only that, but when you think win-lose, the other party has no reason to work with you — he/she will be pitting against you, to "win" over you. He/She sees you as the enemy, while you see him/her as the enemy — and that's not going to create the best outcome for everyone.

The battle isn't against your opponent — it's the conflict. If you are frustrated with your boss, talk to him/her and find a way to match both your needs. If you're angry with your partner, don't try to make things difficult using passive-aggressive methods. Talk to him/her and work out your differences, so that both of you can achieve your goals together. If you're angry with your friend but you want to preserve the friendship, let him/her know your struggles in the friendship and find a solution that works for you and him/her.

Adopt this win-win mindset for conflicts with anyone. Ask yourself: "What is the scenario where everyone will be happy? What is the scenario where everyone will win?" Then work towards that outcome.

4) Have an open discussion

(Image: Matus Laslofi)

An important part of achieving a win-win is to **have an open discussion**. When we act based on our vision of success, we shut the other person out without listening to what they have to say. **Respect that the other person has views and goals that may be different from ours.** To achieve a win-win, hear them out and discuss the best outcome for both of you.

During one of my coaching calls with my client P, she revealed that she has been feeling resentment toward her husband as she has been giving so much to the family: working, taking care of the kids, and doing housework. She feels that she has put her ideal life on hold in caring for the family, without much help from him.

This was a surprising revelation to her as she wasn't consciously thinking this way: it just came out during our call. She still loves her husband and they are sweethearts who have been married for over 10 years; this was simply an issue that had been brewing for a while.

So I asked my client P, "Does he know? Have you ever talked to him about this?"

"No," she said.

I encouraged her to talk to her husband about this, which she did. By the next call, she shared that **they had a very in-depth discussion in a way they don't usually have** and that her husband was surprised to learn about her feelings. He reaffirmed his care and support for her and they agreed to find ways to earn more money and share the household responsibility, rather than letting her take all the burden. **This subsequently brought them closer together.**

On the other hand, if she hadn't had an open talk with her husband, perhaps she might have reacted passive-aggressively such as picking fights, being argumentative, and doing things her way. This would have created more conflicts, made him unhappy, and created a negative household for her, her husband, and their kids. Her husband would still be clueless as to what is going on, and the original conflict would remain unsolved. In the end, everyone loses.

Here are some tips to have an open discussion:

1. **Seek to understand.** Everyone has different views. Understand what they are. Don't override their opinions just because they are different from yours. Understand the other person is thinking and why he/she thinks that way.

2. **Share your views** and **let the person share theirs**. Bridge the divide by sharing your thoughts first. Then, invite the person to share their views. Ensure that each of you has an equal chance to share your views, ask questions, and understand each other.

3. **Be supportive** as the other person is sharing their views. Nod, acknowledge what they are saying, and thank them.

4. **Brainstorm the best solution.** Make it clear that you care about them and that you want to create a win-win outcome for everyone. Work together to identify the best solution, with both your needs in mind.

5) Ground yourself in high consciousness (Don't get angry)

Once you decide to engage in the battle, ground yourself in high consciousness to achieve the best outcome for both of you. **Remember, your goal is to achieve a win-win, not to bring your "opponent" down.** The enemy here is the conflict, not the person.

Yet during a conflict, it can be hard to remain conscious. Sometimes emotions run high and you may say things that you don't mean. Unaired grievances may come up. You may feel like attacking the other person even if you logically know that this isn't the goal. You may also feel like abandoning this battle if the person is not cooperative.

I have some tips to manage this:

1. Before you enter into battle, imagine you're in a calm, peaceful place. No one can hurt you or take you away from this place unless you let them.

2. If there are hurtful words hurled at you, try to engage in a peaceful way. Say, "I understand you are angry, but let's keep this civil. I want to achieve the best outcome for both of us, so let's work together to achieve it."

3. If you feel that you are losing your cool, stop talking to yourself. Imagine you are in a different place and you're here to successfully carry out this discussion. This quote by Rene Des

6) Have an exit point

All battles can be won if we have unlimited resources. The reality though is that we don't have unlimited resources. We can't spend forever working on a problem if it's not progressing despite our best effort.

Have an exit point where you say, "Okay, that's it. Time to cut my losses and move on." This is the point where you exit the battle because you have incurred your maximum loss and you don't want to invest any more time or energy into this.

7) Let go of unresolved battles

If the problem remains unresolved despite your best effort, let it go. **Success comes not from not winning every battle, but learning to let go when it's time to do**

so. While Tip #6 is about knowing when to exit when things don't go your way, this Tip #7 is about **letting go**. Just because you stop fighting a problem doesn't mean that you have let go of it mentally.

Once my friend was having conflicts with her boss and co-workers. They kept talking behind her back, backstabbing her and giving her issues. The environment was cliquish and she didn't fit in.

While she felt deeply troubled and even cried in the office at one point, she later focused on the next steps for her career instead. She worked on her resume and started looking for new jobs. Eventually, she found a job with better pay and work conditions. She has since been working there for two years and is enjoying her work and co-workers. If she had focused on feeling unhappy and angry with her co-workers, she would never have found her new job.

How can you let go?

1. **Acknowledge your feelings.** So things didn't go your way. How do you feel? Sad? Angry? Disappointed? Write down your feelings. Use my brain-dumping exercise to release your emotions.

2. **Understand why you are feeling this way.** There's a reason why you feel aggrieved. Why do you feel this way? What do you feel unjust about? Dig into the root issue. Maybe you feel disrespected. Maybe the situation brings up one of your fears. Maybe the situation deals with something that matters a lot to you. Uncovering the

root issue will help you understand and let go.

3. **Work on a new path forward.** Since the conflict can't be resolved to your satisfaction, how can you move forward? Identify new ways to move forward. With my friend, she couldn't resolve the conflict with her boss and co-workers, and hence the next best step was to look for a new job — which worked out great for her. How can you stay on track in your life plan, despite the battle not turning out the way you want?

In essence, effective decision-making is not just about making choices; it's about making choices that matter. It's about aligning decisions with what truly resonates with your values, aspirations, and well-being—a pivotal aspect of mastering the art of mindful priorities.

Chapter 5

Honesty and Authenticity: Embracing Your True Self

Being true to yourself means living in alignment with your values, beliefs, and personal identity. Living authentically means you do not conform to societal expectations or pretend to be someone you are not. Instead, you embrace who you really are and live your life as an expression of the real you. Being authentic allows you to express your true self, embrace your uniqueness, and honor your individuality. Genuine people possess a quality that sets them apart - they are sincere in their thoughts, actions, and interactions with others.

Society increasingly values appearance over substance. There is so much emphasis on material possessions, how you look, where you vacation, etc. It is almost as if we have forgotten the value of being a genuine person.

The Advantage of Being Authentic

Genuine people embody qualities and live in a way that reflects their inner truth. They embrace authenticity not as a fleeting trend but as a way of life. This brings numerous benefits to their mental health. It also enriches their personal and interpersonal experiences.

SELF-AWARENESS

Authenticity requires self-reflection and a deep understanding of your own values, strengths, weaknesses, and passions. Delving into the process of self-discovery helps you develop a clearer sense of who you are and what you want from life. Genuine individuals engage in introspection. They examine their thoughts, emotions, and motivations. By understanding their own intentions, they can better navigate the world and form fulfilling connections with others.

EMBRACING SELF-ACCEPTANCE

At the core of being a genuine person lies self-acceptance. People that are authentic recognize and embrace their strengths, weaknesses, and quirks. By accepting themselves fully, they develop a deep sense of self-worth. This gives them the ability to engage with the world from a place of authenticity.

CONFIDENCE AND EMPOWERMENT

Embracing your authenticity boosts self-confidence. It empowers you to make choices and decisions that align with your core being. You can take ownership of your life and be true to your values. This leads to a sense of fulfillment and satisfaction. Remember, authenticity is not about being perfect, but about embracing your true self and sharing your unique voice with the world.

INTEGRITY AND HONESTY

Authentic people exhibit integrity and honesty in their words and actions. They align their behavior with their values and beliefs. This builds trust and credibility in their relationships. They have a real desire to communicate transparently and build meaningful connections.

EMBRACING VULNERABILITY

Authenticity and vulnerability go hand in hand. Genuine individuals embrace vulnerability as a strength. They are confident enough in themselves to express their worries, fears, or pain.

HAVING MEANINGFUL RELATIONSHIPS

Being genuine attracts like-minded individuals who appreciate realness. By being authentically you, you will be able to forge deep and meaningful relationships. The value add of keeping it real is that these connections will be based on trust, respect, and mutual understanding. Your relationships will be a space where others can be their true selves, feel accepted, and learn from each other. Enhancing intimacy in relationships is smoother when you are coming from a place of sincerity.

MENTAL AND EMOTIONAL WELL-BEING

Authenticity promotes inner harmony and reduces the anxiety that can arise from living a life that does not align with your true self. When you embrace authenticity, you experience a greater sense of self-acceptance, contentment, and overall well-being. You feel less stress when you are free to be yourself and are comfortable in your skin.

Embracing Your Uniqueness

This is part of self-acceptance, self-approval, and self-love.

Invest some time and energy exploring what your passions, interests, strengths and weaknesses are. This can give you revealing insight into parts of your personality and identity that you may not be aware of. What is it about your point of view or talents that makes you different from others? What are your qualities, skills, or experiences that make you stand out? Understanding what makes you will instill confidence in sharing your thoughts, opinions, and ideas.

Once you embrace your own individuality, you will find that you are more tolerant of the differences in others. Engage with people from different cultures and backgrounds. Make a space for yourself by spending time with people that value diversity and individual expression. This will broaden not only your understanding of society, but also of yourself.

Authenticity in a Digital Age: Navigating the Influence of Social Media

Social media platforms have become an integral part of our lives, shaping how we connect, share, and present ourselves to the world. But carefully curated profiles, presenting only the best or doctored parts of people's lives just add to the sense of inauthenticity.

On social media people often present an idealized version of their reality. Users share their best highlights, reels, and photos of their lives. This can create the illusion that everyone is better off than you. It can cause feelings of inadequacy, especially among the youth.

The pressure to update and maintain an engaging online presence is constant. For many young people, self-worth and esteem now come from how many likes and comments they get on a post instead of from within. The concept of being yourself is lost in the sea of filters and staged moments.

Recognizing the inconsistency between reality and curated content is necessary for embracing authenticity.

Sustaining Genuineness in Kids and Teenagers

Youngsters, particularly adolescents, can be under enormous strain to adjust and fit in. Helping them find and acknowledge what their identity is a significant part of their turn of events. Urge kids and adolescents to communicate their actual selves. This will empower them to fabricate serious areas of strength for self-acknowledgement and certainty. The following are instances of how we can do this.

CREATE A CONDITIONAL FOR ACCEPTANCE

The foundation for children's self-acceptance is their caregivers' validation, acceptance, and approval. Empowering legitimacy starts with establishing a protected and tolerating climate at home, school, and in other group environments. Youngsters and adolescents need to feel open to offering their viewpoints, feelings, and distinction unafraid of judgment or dismissal. By emphasizing the significance of individuality, you can encourage self-acceptance and self-love. Help kids and adolescents to feel happy with embracing their uniqueness, and model how you acknowledge yours. Along these lines, they will foster an appreciation for their assets, interests, and contrasts.

Be an example of respect for different points of view, active listening, and open communication. This will develop a climate that celebrates validness. Training youngsters to commend variety will show them that everybody's bona fide self deserve love and regard.

SELF-Revelation AND SELF-Articulation

Advance self-revelation by empowering youngsters and teenagers to investigate their inclinations, interests, and values. Give open doors to them to participate in many exercises, permitting them to find their extraordinary abilities and qualities. Open them to craftsmanship, books, music, or other inventive outlets. Give them a place where they can express themselves fully.

Embracing your uniqueness frequently requires leaving your usual range of familiarity. Support kids in attempting new things and having fluctuated encounters. This will assist them with revealing features of their character and assets that they didn't know about. This is one more extraordinary opportunity for you to show conduct. Recognize and commend their accomplishments, endeavors, and endeavors.

MODEL Legitimacy

Kids and youngsters gain some useful knowledge by noticing and impersonating others. In our own lives, as parents, educators, and mentors, we must demonstrate authenticity. Allow them to see your actual self. Share your successes and challenges (to the appropriate extent).

Credibility remains inseparable with compassion and regard for other people and oneself. Help youngsters and teenagers to esteem and value alternate points of view, societies, and encounters. Urge them to listen effectively and sympathetically to other people. They cultivate genuine connections and an inclusive mindset by cultivating these qualities. At the point when kids see you rehearsing self-empathy and benevolence towards yourself, they might assimilate these positive qualities.

Tolerating Slip-ups AND Imperfections

Youngsters ought to comprehend that committing errors and it is regular and affirm to have flaws. To construct a development mentality, where disappointments are viewed as learning valuable open doors, you really want to eliminate the component of disgrace. By reminding children that their worth is not based on how they look or what they have accomplished, you can help them develop resilience and self-compassion. Get some information about the pieces of themselves that they might stifle.

Prevailing burdens

Assist kids and adolescents with exploring prevailing difficulties by advancing decisive reasoning and mindfulness. Help them to address cultural standards and assumptions that might go against their real selves. Attempt the thoughts depicted beneath. Keep in mind, with youngsters, having only one discussion isn't sufficient. You should rehash the same thing, audit ideas with kids, and reliably model the conduct you maintain that they should copy.

Explain values and convictions

Have an open discussion about your family's qualities and convictions. Recognize the standards and beliefs that will assist with directing your youngsters' choices and that will shape their perspective. Consult with your kid about what the accompanying mean to them:

Kindness, bravery, happiness, self-worth, being who you are, living honestly, and their personality are all aspects of external pressure.

Instead of giving in to peer pressure or other influences, encourage young people to make decisions that are in line with their values. Reassure children that it is acceptable for them to inquire about their peers' choices. Converse with your youngsters about the convictions they hold. Have they embraced thought and ways of behaving in view of the gathering they are a piece of? Which of these are not really them? How might they relinquish it? Youngsters that vibe secure in what their identity is and a big motivator for they will feel more certain about rising up to peer pressure.

Consider the impact that each young person's morals or beliefs have on their lives. What effect does it have on their overall health? How can it cause them to feel about themselves? Show how important and valuable meaningful connections are. Discuss the connections in your own existence with individuals that motivate and elevate you.

Online entertainment

Have continuous discussions with your youngsters about web-based entertainment. Investigate the subject of careful commitment. This implies surveying who and what they are interfacing with on the web. Is there any worth add - either from their end or from the record/individual they are drawing in with? Show them instances of positive and valuable discussions that help others' real articulation. It is difficult to draw in without examination or judgment, yet with the right rules and practice, children can arrive.

As readers immerse themselves in "The Art of Mindful Priorities," this chapter becomes a mirror reflecting the incongruence between societal expectations and personal truths. It's an awakening—an illumination of the power found in authenticity and the transformative ripple effect it creates.

Those who journey through these pages will find themselves emboldened to traverse the world with unbridled authenticity. They'll recognize the beauty in their vulnerabilities and the strength in their authenticity.

This chapter isn't just a call to embrace one's true self; it's an awakening to the reality that authenticity is not a flaw but a radiant beacon guiding us toward a more fulfilling and genuine existence.

Chapter 6

Detaching from Outcomes: Finding Peace in Acceptance

"Detaching from Outcomes: Finding Peace in Acceptance" invites us into the serene realm of letting go—the art of relinquishing our grip on specific results and embracing the beauty of surrender.

In a world driven by the pursuit of predefined outcomes, the notion of detachment often feels counterintuitive.

However, this chapter heralds the profound wisdom that lies in detaching ourselves from the strings of desired outcomes.

This journey begins with understanding that our efforts and intentions are within

our control, while outcomes often reside beyond our grasp. It's an acknowledgment that despite meticulous planning and dedication, life is inherently unpredictable, and certain variables remain beyond our influence.

1. Embracing the Art of Detachment

Detachment, often misunderstood as indifference or apathy, is an art that holds immense power in our pursuit of inner peace and emotional well-being. It involves consciously distancing ourselves from the outcomes, opinions, and attachments that often cause us stress and anxiety. By embracing the art of detachment, we can learn to navigate life's challenges with a sense of calm and clarity. In this blog post, we will delve deeper into the concept of detachment, exploring its benefits, providing practical tips, and examining **real-life case studies** to illustrate its transformative effects.

2. Understanding Detachment: What it is and What it is Not

Detachment is not about disconnecting from our emotions or shutting ourselves off from the world. Instead, it is a conscious choice to observe and accept our emotions without allowing them to control us. It is about cultivating a sense of inner peace that remains unaffected by external circumstances or the opinions of others. Detachment allows us to maintain our equanimity in the face of challenges, enabling us to respond rather than react impulsively.

3. The Benefits of Detachment: Finding Freedom and Inner Peace

By embracing detachment, we free ourselves from the burden of expectations, attachments, and the need for validation. This newfound freedom allows us to experience life fully, without being weighed down by the constant desire for control or the fear of disappointment. Detachment empowers us to let go of the need to change others or situations beyond our control, allowing us to focus on our own growth and well-being.

4. Tips for Cultivating Detachment in Daily Life

A) Practice mindfulness: Mindfulness meditation can help us observe our thoughts and emotions without judgment, allowing us to detach from them and gain a broader perspective.

B) Let go of attachments: Identify attachments that cause you stress and consciously work on releasing them. This could be attachments to outcomes, material possessions, or even relationships that no longer serve you.

C) Cultivate self-awareness: Pay attention to your emotional responses and triggers. By understanding what triggers you and why, you can consciously choose to detach from those triggers and respond in a more balanced manner.

5. Case Studies: Real-Life Examples of the Transformative Power of Detachment

A) Sarah, a working professional, was constantly stressed and anxious about meeting the expectations of her demanding job. Through therapy and practicing detachment, she learned to focus on doing her best without attaching her self-worth to external achievements. This shift allowed her to find greater peace and fulfillment in her work.

B) Mark struggled with a fear of rejection, which prevented him from pursuing his passion for writing. By detaching from the fear of judgment, he started sharing his work online, receiving positive feedback and gaining confidence in his abilities.

Embracing the art of detachment can bring about profound positive changes in our lives. It allows us to navigate challenges with grace, find inner peace, and live more authentically. By understanding what detachment truly means and implementing practical tips, we can cultivate this invaluable skill and experience the transformative power it holds.

1. A Path to Inner Peace

Detachment is often misunderstood as a cold and unfeeling state of being. However, in reality, it is a powerful tool that can lead to inner peace and harmony. By learning to detach ourselves from our thoughts, emotions, and external circumstances, we can cultivate a sense of neutrality and find solace in the present moment. In this section, we will explore the concept of detachment and delve into its practical applications for finding peace in our lives.

2. Letting go of attachments

One of the fundamental aspects of detachment is letting go of attachments. Attachments can take various forms, such as clinging to expectations, possessions, relationships, or even our own self-image. These attachments create a sense of dependency and prevent us from experiencing true freedom and inner peace. By recognizing our attachments and consciously choosing to let go of them, we can create space for new possibilities and open ourselves up to a deeper sense of peace.

3. . Observing without judgment

Detachment also involves observing our thoughts, emotions, and external circumstances without judgment. Often, we become entangled in our own narratives and judgments, which can lead to unnecessary suffering. By cultivating a non-judgmental attitude, we can detach ourselves from the need to control or change our experiences. Instead, we can simply observe them as they arise and pass away, allowing us to find peace in the midst of chaos.

4. . Embracing impermanence

Another key aspect of detachment is embracing the impermanence of life. Everything in this world is in a constant state of flux, and holding onto things or people as if they will last forever only leads to disappointment and suffering. By accepting the transient nature of life, we can detach ourselves from the need for permanence and find peace in embracing the present moment. This doesn't mean we should avoid forming deep connections or pursuing our goals, but rather that we should hold them lightly and appreciate the beauty of impermanence.

5. Case study: Esther journey to detachment

Esther, a young professional, found herself constantly stressed and overwhelmed by the demands of her job. She would often bring work home, unable to detach herself from the pressures of her career. As a result, her personal relationships suffered, and she felt a constant sense of restlessness. Recognizing the need for change, Esther started practicing detachment by setting boundaries between work and personal life. She began to prioritize self-care and found solace in engaging in activities that brought her joy. Gradually, Esther's stress levels decreased, and she experienced a newfound sense of inner peace.

6. . Tips for cultivating detachment

- Practice mindfulness and meditation to develop awareness of your thoughts and emotions.

- Take regular breaks from technology and external distractions to reconnect with yourself.

- Cultivate gratitude for the present moment and appreciate the simple joys in life.

- Surround yourself with supportive and like-minded individuals who encourage detachment.

- Practice self-compassion and embrace self-care as an essential part of your well-being.

Detachment is a lifelong journey that requires patience and practice. By consciously choosing to detach ourselves from attachments, observing without judgment, embracing impermanence, and learning from case studies like Sarah's, we can gradually find peace within ourselves and navigate life's challenges with greater equanimity.

3. Releasing Attachments and Expectations

- Identify and acknowledge your attachments and expectations

The first step in letting go and releasing attachments and expectations is to become aware of what they are. Take some time to reflect on the areas of your life where you feel a strong sense of attachment or expectation. It could be in relationships, career, material possessions, or even in your own self-image. By identifying these attachments and expectations, you can begin to understand the impact they have on your life and well-being.

- Understand the nature of attachments and expectations

Attachments and expectations are often rooted in fear, insecurity, or a need for control. We hold onto things or people because we believe they bring us happiness, security, or validation. Similarly, we have expectations of how things should be or how people should act, based on our own desires and beliefs.

However, it's important to recognize that attachments and expectations can hold us back and prevent us from experiencing true freedom and inner peace.

- Practice non-attachment and acceptance

Once you have identified your attachments and expectations, it's time to start practicing non-attachment and acceptance. This doesn't mean that you have to give up on your desires or stop setting goals. Instead, it's about cultivating a mindset of detachment and letting go of the need for things to be a certain way. It's about accepting the present moment as it is, without clinging to the past or worrying about the future.

For example, if you have a strong attachment to a particular outcome in your career, such as getting a promotion, try to detach yourself from the outcome and focus on doing your best in the present moment. Accept that there are factors beyond your control and that the outcome may not always align with your expectations. By letting go of attachment and embracing acceptance, you open yourself up to new possibilities and opportunities.

4. Navigating Life's Ups and Downs

1. Recognizing the Power of Emotional Neutrality

In the ever-changing landscape of life, it is inevitable that we will encounter a range of emotions, both positive and negative. While it is natural to experience joy during moments of success and happiness, it is equally common to feel sadness, frustration, or anger when faced with challenges or setbacks. However, cultivating emotional neutrality can provide us with a powerful tool to navigate life's ups and downs with grace and resilience.

2. Understanding Emotional Neutrality

Emotional neutrality refers to a state of mind where we detach ourselves from the intense emotions that often accompany certain situations. It does not mean suppressing or denying our feelings, but rather observing them without judgment or attachment. By adopting this perspective, we can gain a clearer understanding of our emotions and make more rational decisions, free from the influence of strong emotional reactions.

3. Embracing the Middle Ground

One of the fundamental aspects of emotional neutrality is finding the middle ground between extreme emotional states. For example, when faced with disappointment, rather than succumbing to despair or becoming overly optimistic, we can strive to maintain a balanced perspective. By acknowledging our disappointment while also recognizing that setbacks are a natural part of life, we can cultivate emotional resilience and keep moving forward.

4. Practicing Mindfulness

Mindfulness is a powerful practice that can help us cultivate emotional neutrality. By being fully present in the moment and observing our thoughts and emotions non-judgment

5. Balancing Love and Independence

1. Finding the right balance in relationships can be a delicate art, especially when it comes to the concept of detachment. Detachment in relationships refers to maintaining a sense of individuality and independence while still nurturing a deep bond with your partner. It involves striking a harmonious balance between love and independence, allowing both partners to grow and thrive while maintaining a strong

connection. In this section, we will delve into the importance of detachment in relationships and explore some practical tips for achieving this delicate balance.

2. One key aspect of detachment in relationships is the ability to maintain a sense of self. It is crucial to remember that while being in a relationship, each individual has their own dreams, goals, and personal space. It is essential to respect and support each other's individuality, allowing room for personal growth and exploration. For example, encouraging your partner to pursue their hobbies or interests, even if they differ from your own, can foster a sense of independence and personal fulfillment.

3. Communication plays a vital role in achieving detachment in relationships. Open and honest communication allows both partners to express their needs, desires, and boundaries. By discussing expectations and setting healthy boundaries, individuals can maintain their independence without jeopardizing the relationship. Case studies have shown that couples who communicate effectively and openly tend to have stronger relationships, as they are better able to understand and respect each other's need for independence.

4. Another important aspect of detachment in relationships is the ability to cultivate a healthy sense of interdependence. Interdependence refers to the mutual reliance and support

between partners, where both individuals contribute to the relationship while still maintaining their independence. This can be achieved through shared responsibilities, mutual decision-making, and a willingness to compromise. For instance, taking turns in making important decisions or dividing household chores can help foster a sense of equality and balance in the relationship.

5. It is crucial to recognize that detachment does not mean emotional disengagement or indifference. Instead, it involves finding a middle ground between being overly dependent and emotionally distant. It is important to strike a balance between being emotionally available and having the freedom to pursue personal

growth. This can be achieved by nurturing your own emotional well-being through self-care practices such as meditation, journaling, or pursuing hobbies that bring you joy.

6. Finally, it is essential to remember that detachment in relationships is a continuous process that requires ongoing effort and commitment from both partners. It is normal for couples to face challenges along the way, but by practicing empathy, understanding, and patience, individuals can navigate these challenges while maintaining a healthy balance between love and independence. Regular check-ins and open conversations about the state of the relationship can help ensure that

both partners feel heard, understood, and supported.

Detachment in relationships is a delicate balancing act that requires individuals to maintain their sense of self while nurturing a deep connection with their partner. By fostering open communication, respecting each other's individuality, and cultivating a healthy sense of interdependence, couples can achieve a harmonious balance between love and independence. So, embrace the art of detachment and find peace in neutrality as you navigate the beautiful journey of relationships.

6. Embracing the Present Moment

☐ Acceptance is a powerful tool that allows us to find peace and contentment in the present moment. It involves acknowledging and embracing our current circumstances, whether they are positive or negative, without judgment or resistance. By practicing acceptance, we can let go of the need to control or change our reality, and instead focus on finding inner peace and happiness. In this section, we will explore the power of acceptance and how it can help us embrace the present moment.

☐ One of the key aspects of acceptance is understanding that we cannot change the past or predict the future. We often waste precious energy and mental space by dwelling on past mistakes or worrying about what might happen in the future. By accepting the present moment as it is, we free ourselves from the burden of regret and anxiety. We can focus on what we can control and take steps towards a positive future, rather than being consumed by what we cannot change.

☐ Acceptance also allows us to cultivate gratitude for the present moment, even in challenging times. When we accept our circumstances, we open ourselves up to finding beauty and joy in the simplest of things. For example, instead of resenting a rainy day, we can appreciate the soothing sound of raindrops or the opportunity to cozy up with a good book. By shifting our perspective and accepting what is, we can find happiness and contentment in even the most ordinary moments.

☐ Case Study: Sarah was a high-achieving professional who constantly pushed herself to reach new goals and milestones. She believed that happiness and fulfillment would come once she achieved certain external markers of success. However, despite her accomplishments, Sarah found herself feeling empty and unsatisfied. Through therapy, she learned the power of acceptance and began to shift her focus to the present moment. As she embraced her current circumstances and let go of the need for external validation, Sarah found a newfound sense of peace and contentment. She started to appreciate the small joys in life and prioritize her own well-being, ultimately leading to a more fulfilling and meaningful existence.

☐ Tips for practicing acceptance:

A. Cultivate mindfulness: Mindfulness is the practice of being fully present and aware of our thoughts, emotions, and sensations in the present moment. By cultivating mindfulness, we can become more attuned to our experiences and develop a greater sense of acceptance.

B. Practice self-compassion: Acceptance starts with being kind and compassionate towards ourselves. Instead of judging or criticizing ourselves for our perceived flaws or mistakes, we can practice self-compassion and embrace our imperfections.

C. Let go of control: Acceptance involves surrendering the need to control every aspect of our lives. Recognize that there are certain things beyond your control and focus on what you can influence or change.

D. Seek support: If you find it challenging to practice acceptance on your own, consider seeking support from a therapist or joining a support group. Sharing your experiences and learning from others can be incredibly helpful in cultivating acceptance.

☐ Embracing the power of acceptance can transform our lives and bring us closer to a state of inner peace. By accepting the present moment, we can let go of unnecessary stress, find gratitude in the simplest of things, and live a more fulfilling and meaningful life. Remember, acceptance is not about resignation or giving up, but rather about embracing what is and finding peace in neutrality.

☐ Finding Freedom in Minimalism

● The allure of material possessions has always been deeply ingrained in our society. We are constantly bombarded with advertisements and social pressures to accumulate more and more things. However, as many people are beginning to realize, the pursuit of material possessions often leads to a never-ending cycle of desire and dissatisfaction. In recent years, a growing movement called minimalism has gained traction, advocating for a simpler and more intentional way of living. Detaching from material possessions and embracing minimalism can bring about a sense of freedom and contentment that is often elusive in our consumer-driven culture.

- One of the key principles of minimalism is decluttering. By getting rid of unnecessary possessions, we create space for what truly matters in our lives. This process can be both liberating and transformative. Take a look around your home and ask yourself: Do I really need all these clothes, gadgets, or knick-knacks? Embracing minimalism means letting go of the excess and focusing on what adds value to our lives. Case studies have shown that decluttering can lead to reduced stress levels, increased productivity, and improved mental well-being.

- Another aspect of detaching from material possessions is embracing a more sustainable and conscious lifestyle. Minimalism encourages us to be mindful of the environmental impact of our consumption habits. By reducing our reliance on material goods, we minimize waste and contribute to a healthier planet. For example, instead of buying new clothing items every season, we can opt for a minimalist wardrobe consisting of versatile and timeless pieces. This not only saves money in the long run but also reduces the demand for fast fashion, which is notorious for its negative environmental and ethical implications.

- Detaching from material possessions also allows us to shift our focus from accumulating things to cultivating experiences and relationships. Instead of spending our hard-earned money on the latest gadgets or luxury items, we can invest in activities that bring us joy and fulfillment. This might involve traveling to new places, pursuing hobbies, or simply spending quality time with loved ones. By prioritizing experiences over material possessions, we create lasting memories and find true happiness in the intangible aspects of life.

- Tips for embracing minimalism and detaching from material possessions:

- Start small: Begin by decluttering one area of your home or one category of items, such as clothing or books. This will help you build momentum and make the process more manageable.

- Practice gratitude: Appreciate the things you already have and focus on their value rather than constantly seeking more.

- Set boundaries: Resist the urge to mindlessly consume by establishing rules for yourself, such as a one-in, one-out policy or a spending limit.

- Seek support: connect with like-minded individuals who are also on a minimalist journey. Share experiences, tips, and challenges to stay motivated and inspired.

Detaching from material possessions and embracing minimalism can lead to a more fulfilling and intentional way of living. By decluttering, adopting a sustainable mindset, and prioritizing experiences over things, we can find freedom from the never-ending pursuit of more. Ultimately, minimalism is not about deprivation, but rather about discovering what truly matters and living a life aligned with our values.

8. Achieving Goals without Losing Yourself
  • Understand the Concept of Detachment

Detachment is often misunderstood as a lack of interest or apathy towards one's goals. However, in reality, detachment is about finding a balance between ambition and inner peace. It is about pursuing success without becoming consumed by it. When we detach ourselves from the outcome of our goals, we can approach them with a clear and calm mind, allowing us to make better decisions and enjoy the journey towards success.

- Embrace the Process, Not Just the Outcome

One of the key aspects of detachment is learning to embrace the process rather than solely focusing on the end result. When we become too fixated on achieving a particular outcome, we tend to overlook the valuable lessons and experiences that come along the way. By detaching ourselves from the desired outcome, we can fully immerse ourselves in the present moment and appreciate the growth and learning that occurs throughout the journey. For example, if your goal is to start a successful business, instead of solely focusing on the end result, embrace the challenges, failures, and small victories that come with building a business from scratch.

- Find Inner Fulfillment

Detachment allows us to find fulfillment within ourselves rather than relying on external achievements for happiness. When we attach our self-worth solely to our goals, we become vulnerable to feelings of emptiness and dissatisfaction if we fail to achieve them. On the other hand, detaching ourselves from the outcome enables us to find joy and contentment in the process, regardless of the final outcome. Take time to identify activities or practices that bring you inner peace and fulfillment, such as meditation, journaling, or spending time in nature. Cultivating these habits will help you maintain a sense of self even amidst the pursuit of your goals.

- Maintain Perspective

Detachment helps us maintain a broader perspective on life and our goals. When we are too attached to our goals, setbacks and obstacles can feel overwhelming and insurmountable. However, by detaching ourselves from the outcome, we can approach challenges with a calm and rational mindset. It allows us to see setbacks as opportunities for growth and learning, rather than as failures. For instance, if you encounter a setback in your career, instead of dwelling on the disappointment, detach yourself from the negative emotions and explore how you can learn from the experience and make improvements.

- Case Study: Elon Musk

Elon Musk, the visionary entrepreneur behind SpaceX and Tesla, provides a compelling case study on detachment and success. Despite his ambitious goals and relentless pursuit of innovation, Musk maintains a level of detachment from the outcomes. He recognizes that failure is a part of the process and has often stated that he is willing to fail if it means pushing the boundaries of what is possible. This detachment allows him to stay focused on his goals without losing himself in the pursuit of success.

Detachment and success go hand in hand. By understanding the concept of detachment, embracing the process, finding inner fulfillment, maintaining perspective, and drawing inspiration from successful individuals like Elon Musk, we can achieve our goals without losing ourselves along the way. Detachment empowers us to approach our ambitions with clarity, resilience, and a sense of peace.

9. Embracing Detachment as a Lifelong Journey

☐ Letting go of attachments and embracing detachment is not a one-time event, but rather a lifelong journey. It requires constant self-awareness, practice, and a willingness to let go of our ego-driven desires and expectations. Detachment is not about disconnecting from life or becoming indifferent; it is about finding inner peace and freedom by releasing our attachment to outcomes and external circumstances. In this concluding section, we will explore the importance of embracing detachment as a lifelong journey and provide some practical tips to help you on this path.

☐ One of the key aspects of embracing detachment is learning to let go of control. We often hold on tightly to our plans, expectations, and desires, believing that we have control over the outcome. However, life is unpredictable, and trying to control every aspect of it only leads to frustration and disappointment. By accepting that we cannot control everything, we open ourselves up to new possibilities and opportunities. This does not mean that we should stop setting goals or working towards them; rather, it means being open to detours and unexpected outcomes that may ultimately lead us to a better place.

☐ Another important aspect of embracing detachment is cultivating a mindset of non-attachment. This involves recognizing that everything in life is impermanent and constantly changing. Our attachments to people, possessions, and even our own identities can cause suffering when we cling to them too tightly. By letting go of our attachments, we create space for growth, transformation, and new experiences. For example, instead of defining ourselves solely by our careers or relationships, we can embrace the idea that we are constantly evolving beings with the capacity to explore different paths and possibilities.

☐ Practicing mindfulness is a powerful tool in the journey of detachment. Mindfulness allows us to observe our thoughts, emotions, and attachments without judgment or attachment. By **cultivating a present-moment awareness**, we can detach ourselves from the stories and narratives we create in our minds. This practice helps us to become more aware of our attachments and enables us to let go of them with greater ease. Through mindfulness, we can develop a sense of inner peace and clarity that transcends the ups and downs of external circumstances.

☐ Case studies have shown that embracing detachment can lead to increased happiness, reduced stress, and improved overall well-being. For instance, research has found that individuals who are less attached to material possessions and external achievements tend to have higher levels of life satisfaction. By shifting their focus from external validation to internal fulfillment, they experience greater contentment and joy. Moreover, embracing detachment can also enhance our relationships, as we become less reliant on others for our happiness and more capable of loving unconditionally.

☐ In conclusion, embracing detachment is not a destination but a lifelong journey. It requires a shift in mindset, a willingness to let go of control, and a commitment to practicing mindfulness. By embracing detachment, we free ourselves from the constraints of attachment and open ourselves up to a life of greater peace, joy, and fulfillment. So, embark on this journey with an open heart and a curious mind, and remember that detachment is not about disconnecting from life, but rather finding freedom within.

Chapter 7

Cultivating Resilience: Thriving Amidst Challenges

In the excursion of self-improvement, flexibility assumes a crucial part in defeating difficulties and exploring through life's high points and low points. The force of flexibility, with its capacity to help us quickly return and adjust, is a key expertise that pushes us forward.

With their mastery and experiences, proficient speakers shed light on the meaning of strength and tell the best way to develop this fundamental quality. Through their provocative talks and persuasive introductions, they rouse people to embrace flexibility, overcome snags, and flourish in misfortune. With the guidance of professional speakers, you can discover the transformative power of resilience and unlock your growth potential.

Figuring out Versatility

Flexibility is a strong characteristic that permits people to return from difficulties, adjust to change, and flourish in difficulty. We begin to comprehend strong individuals' attributes as we further research the possibility of flexibility. Best powerful orator shed light on these characteristics, featuring the significance of strength in private and expert development.

Assurance, constancy, and the ability to keep an uplifting perspective in the midst of attempting conditions are qualities of versatile individuals. They solidly trust in their ability to beat provokes and consider disappointments to be opportunities to progress. We can all the more likely handle the changing capability of versatility in conquering hindrances and making progress by checking its benefits out.

Also, the science behind flexibility dives into the neurological and mental parts of versatility. The most powerful orator demonstrate the way that flexibility can be fabricated and reinforced through logical information. They give valuable tips to further develop strength by revealing insight into the mind's ability to change and revamp itself in light of affliction.

Through convincing talks and energetic introductions, these speakers persuade individuals to make flexibility and understand its true capacity. They share individual stories, contextual analyses, and examination supported strategies to engage crowds to deal with difficulties directly and continue on through troublesome times. The comprehension of versatility acquired from these specialists fills in as an establishment for self-improvement and achievement.

Building Flexibility Abilities
Creating explicit capacities and embracing specific outlooks are key parts of the unique course of building versatility. Famous

motivational speakers as well as business motivational speakers stress how important these skills are for overcoming obstacles and achieving long-term success.

Fostering an uplifting perspective and confidence is an urgent part in upgrading versatility. This involves rewording horrible thoughts, underlining your capacities, and keeping a positive outlook. By developing a positive mentality, people can with certainty approach obstructions and track down arrangements in spite of difficulty.

The ability to appreciate anyone on a profound level and mindfulness are likewise essential in building flexibility. Stressful situations can be handled with resilience and composure by people who understand and control their emotions. Mindfulness empowers individuals to recognize their resources, imperfections, and triggers and change and respond emphatically to troubles.

The capacity to change and be adaptable is one more fundamental quality of versatility. The capacity to embrace change, change systems, and track down elective ways ahead is fundamental in conquering deterrents. Powerful orator for business and notable inspirational orator give tips and deceives for further developing flexibility to make due in always evolving conditions.

People can foster the capacity to recuperate from mishaps, manage vulnerability, and keep on working at an undeniable level by rehearsing these strength characteristics. Business and well known inspirational orators give functional bits of knowledge, apparatuses, and methods to really foster these abilities.

Procedures for Beating Difficulties
It is pivotal to have proficient designs to manage issues. Persuasive speakers stress

the accompanying techniques for beating obstructions and difficulties:

Learning from setbacks and failures: Disappointments can advance development and are viewed as significant learning amazing open doors instead of deterrents. Speakers who inspire listeners to examine their mistakes, draw conclusions, and apply what they learn to future endeavors.

Creating critical thinking and thinking abilities: Individuals who have further developed critical thinking abilities can handle issues with a proactive mentality. Persuasive orator offers valuable techniques and structures for further developing critical thinking and navigation, enabling audience members to deal with testing conditions with affirmation and clearness.

Developing a support system and seeking assistance: Fostering a strong emotionally supportive network is fundamental for strength. Moving speakers stress the benefit of asking others for exhortation, mentorship, and backing. They encourage individuals to encircle themselves with playful and similar individuals who can offer help, direction, and help while managing troubles.

Developing Resilience in a Variety of Settings Resilience is not just about overcoming challenges in one setting. It encompasses a variety of settings. Top business and motivational speakers emphasize the significance of developing resilience in a variety of contexts:

Resilience in interpersonal and social relationships: Flexibility is important for laying out and keeping up with great connections. As per top business speakers, strong associations are encouraged by empathic corporations, powerful correspondence, and compromise. They exhort making strong informal organizations and defeating relational challenges with balance and deftness.

Versatility in the work environment: Versatility in the work environment and in vocation improvement is important to prevail in the quick moving, serious professional workplace. The best persuasive orator shares procedures for overseeing pressure, quickly returning from mishaps, and embracing change in the work environment. They offer guidance on holding a development outlook to prevail over the long haul, handle proficient misfortunes, and make strength in work changes.

Versatility in wellbeing and prosperity: Keeping up with physical and profound prosperity requires strength. Top business speakers underline the significance of taking care of oneself, stress the board, and keeping a positive outlook to explore wellbeing challenges. They offer exhortation on focusing on prosperity, fostering a sound balance between fun and serious activities, and creating versatility despite difficulty.

Individuals can expand their versatility and ability to defeat snags by rehearsing flexibility in these different circles of life. These speakers offer significant techniques, individual encounters, and down to earth apparatuses to engage people to flourish in all parts of their lives, supporting their excursion toward progress and satisfaction.

Sustaining Versatility in Youngsters and Youths
Flexibility is an essential expertise that youngsters and youths can use to explore life's difficulties. Top motivational speakers stress the significance of cultivating young people's resilience.

Their folks and other essential parental figures fundamentally impact youngsters' strength. These speakers stress establishing a sustaining and strong climate that advances independence, critical thinking, and sound gamble taking. Through their actions and attitudes, they instruct on how to encourage open communication, active listening, and resilience.

Kids and teenagers ought to be trained survival strategies to recuperate from mishaps. Proficient speakers underline the significance of teaching kids about pressure the executives, feeling guideline, and defeating impediments. They give useful techniques to building the capacity to understand individuals at their core, for example, care works out, positive self-talk, and sound source for communicating feelings.

Developing a development mentality and encouraging positive confidence are basic for building versatility. Top persuasive orators urge youngsters to take on hardships, gain from botches, and put stock in their capacities to beat obstacles. They encourage individuals to embrace their assets, have a hopeful viewpoint, and lay out a decent mental self view.

Guardians and different grown-ups who care for kids and youths can offer them the certainty and versatility they need to manage life's promising and less promising times by empowering their flexibility. Best powerful orator give important bits of knowledge, functional systems, and moving stories to help guardians and parental figures in cultivating versatility in youthful people, empowering them to flourish and prosper as they develop.

Resilience in the Face of Adversity Resilience in the face of adversity is crucial to one's professional and personal growth. Moving and business powerful orator give important experiences on supporting flexibility.

Flexibility relies upon dealing with oneself. Uplifting speakers underline the significance of taking care of oneself practices like ordinary activity, satisfactory rest, and supporting the psyche and body. They give methods to dealing with pressure well, including care, contemplation, and limit setting to stay balanced.

When confronted with trouble, it is fundamental to formulate solid survival methods. Business persuasive orator guides distinguish powerful survival techniques that line up with individual qualities and values. They teach people how to solve problems, practice problem-solving skills, and engage in activities that are calming and good for their emotions.

Individuals who view hardships as opportunities for development will quite often be stronger. Inspirational orator advance a development mentality by featuring the significance of gaining from botches. They offer counsel on reconsidering misfortunes, tolerating change, and involving disappointments as venturing stones toward accomplishment while sharing individual accounts of beating difficulty.

As readers engage with "The Art of Mindful Priorities," this chapter becomes a reservoir of wisdom—a source of inspiration for those navigating through life's trials. It becomes a testament to the human spirit's resilience and an invitation to rise above challenges, not merely surviving but thriving amidst them.

Those who absorb the teachings of this chapter will find themselves equipped with a resilient mindset—a mindset that transforms obstacles into stepping stones and hardships into opportunities. They'll emerge from the shadows of adversity stronger, wiser, and more empowered, embodying the essence of resilience as they navigate the intricate tapestry of life.

This chapter serves as a guide, empowering individuals to not just weather life's storms but to bloom amidst them, embodying resilience as a beacon of strength and growth.

Chapter 8

Conclusion: Mastering the Art of Mindful Priorities

In the conclusion, "Mastering the Art of Mindful Priorities," we arrive at the culmination of a transformative journey—a journey that invited us to reevaluate our relationship with time, attention, and purpose. It's a synthesis of the wisdom garnered throughout this exploration, encapsulating the essence of intentional living.

The pursuit of mindful priorities isn't a destination but an ongoing journey—a commitment to conscious choices and deliberate living. It's about embracing the power of our decisions and acknowledging that our priorities shape the trajectory of our lives.

Throughout this exploration, we've ventured into the depths of mindful prioritization, challenging the notion that we must care about everything equally. We've discovered the potency of selective attention, unveiling the liberation found in directing our focus toward what truly matters.

We confronted the illusion of perfection, learning to embrace imperfection as a testament to our authenticity. We acknowledged the transformative impact of effective decision-making, realizing that choosing our battles wisely is a reflection of our values and aspirations.

The quest for authenticity led us to unmask our true selves, acknowledging that honesty and authenticity are not weaknesses but manifestations of courage. We discovered the tranquility found in detachment from specific outcomes, understanding that acceptance doesn't equate to resignation but to empowerment.

Finally, we unearthed the resilience dormant within us, recognizing that thriving amidst challenges is not only possible but a testament to our indomitable spirit.

Mastering the art of mindful priorities isn't a solitary endeavor—it's a shared aspiration. It's an invitation to sculpt our lives intentionally, contributing to a world where individuals embrace authenticity, make conscious choices, and navigate challenges with resilience.

As we conclude this journey, let us carry forth the wisdom gained, integrating it into the tapestry of our daily lives. Let us remember that the art of mindful priorities isn't about perfection but about progress, about consistently aligning our actions with our values and aspirations.

May this journey serve as a compass guiding us toward a more intentional, fulfilling existence. May it inspire us to share this wisdom, cultivating a ripple effect of mindful living in our communities and beyond.

In mastering the art of mindful priorities, we discover the profound beauty of intentional living—an existence where our priorities aren't mere items on a checklist but guiding stars illuminating the path to a more purposeful and authentic way of being.